LOVE and LOSS

Gentleman K J

ISBN 978-1-8383550-0-5

© Cover Design Gentleman K J

© Illustrations Gentleman K J

Keekoo Publications

First Published in 2021

Dedicated to four special people
Rich, Mike, Di and Ed

LOVE and LOSS

This collection of poems and images focus on certain strong, emotional experiences. These are now brought into sharp relief by the sudden infection of a virus that keeps those we love separated from us. At the moments of their suffocation and passing we cannot now be with them, to touch and comfort them. The desperate need to be with them is denied.

Must it be at moments of loss we fully realise what we lose?

Starting with thoughts and images of love: and the wonderful, all consuming first love and lasting love, the images and words move through finding love and being loved to the abject distress of loss to considering trying to manage the thoughts and feelings this brings. To share such strong emotions rather than shutting them away could be a way of managing them.

Life and living always moves on. Never to deny such feelings but to appreciate another's life, even celebrate it, in how we continue to live and manage living now, is the best memory of them.

Could not this lost love lead to deeper understanding, support and hope, for others better than self-indulgent grief that separates us from them?

From our thought and actions shall we remember them and ourselves be known.

Darling

Should I say
'I love you'
a hundred times?
As if repetition of our years
was sufficient cause
or perhaps that ache
that awaits your presence
still hides in absence
when we are apart.

I hug your being to me
through all life's weathers.
If sometimes
the ocean of our dreams
seems small:
If in some distant harbour
life closes in, as it must,
my deep love for you
holds still to share and support
and always treasure to the last
that precious love we found
filling our hearts and minds now
as in those many years ago.

In Love

I think and write a dream;
Can it be true as it does seem,
that all my love for you is shared;
Your notes to me so strong,
in your separation
my feelings can't be wrong
but confirm my destination.
Kneeling before the radiance
of your image in mind,
without you life seems grey,
other thoughts left behind
being with you makes my day.
My whole being is moved
by the knowledge of your love,
and my feeble words showed
I am transformed from above,
for you are my sunrise and
my sunset.

Let Us Touch Living

The usual clothes lay in wait for the day
Draped across a chair waiting an arm or two,
to activate the day doing usual things;
Walking, bending about, cleaning, sorting,
smelling, touching, taking things on board
to fit or frustrate small ambitions.

Oh! Let's touch living
in multiple ways;
Touch you, touch me;
Finger tip to full embrace.
Suck sensation back
into life and living.

Love must mean more
than daily chores though
shared with fun and joy.
Who should ask for more
with you beside me singing
before we fold the day away
knowing it's been our way.

The Mirror of Days

These passing days
I look into my ways
through the mirror of
our shared, lasting love
seeking you as ever
for love that fades never.

Managing the way before
became a life we would store;
All we thought we now hold
would be there as we grow old;
The mirror's lustre not denied
where people and events hide.

The chemistry to time will prove
the images that hold our love
for our way ahead not resigned
where love rests in each mind.
This stilted verse, just for you;
always there to see us through
the mirror of our days.

Sometimes

Sometimes I count
the moments of
your passing,
when the sky fell in
and shadows
were everywhere.
The clouded horizons
of my darkened mind
gathered at an ending
that will not leave me.
Out there the grass
still grows, flowers bloom,
birds sing, footsteps
cross my door.
I am mostly normal;
Holding the distress
at losing you, abides;
It still weeps from me
when the world's busy
face is turned away and
I must alone hold you
more than sometimes.

Survival

Routines hold days together
But make memories grey.
The light, colour, connections,
to that vivid life now lost,
fades in the rounds of a busy day.
My route over the distant hill
offers other sorts of living.
Must I away to try another life and
forfeit lived recollections of our days?
Always the hollow in the lost land
can seem a better place to curl
to keep the hurt away.
Even so the daily round,
filling the spaces of the mind,
can bring forgetfulness.
Don't let routine oblivion
reduce your mind-image,
Fog your inner voice,
leave me paralysed without you.
I will never forget you, darling
and our precious life together
that rests still with me when
the clock stops, time stalls,
and I will, at last, be with you.

Thoughts by Your Grave

So I am here, you are there;
Time and events separate us
to the edges of experience
where we must both inhabit
this world as we now find it:
One buried in earth; earth at peace,
No erosions nor time can
erase you from my memory
how ever life finds renewal.

Sitting by your grave,
despite the deep sorrow I feel,
words must find their way
into my pen to hold me still
to celebrate your life in me.
Though breathing in the sadness
of your passing I must remain.
There are hints of Autumn in the trees.
All things pass, some find renewal.

How should I think of or remember you
while sitting here by your grave?
As plants brave an early frost, birds
fill throats with seeds not songs,
plants filling buds ready for renewal.
Perhaps there is circularity here,
for birds' throats to find a new song,
the reformed flower its root and stem;
So I too must find renewal.

Yet we all know there are ends waiting;
waiting some vantage over emptiness.
I then feel you in the essence of renewal.

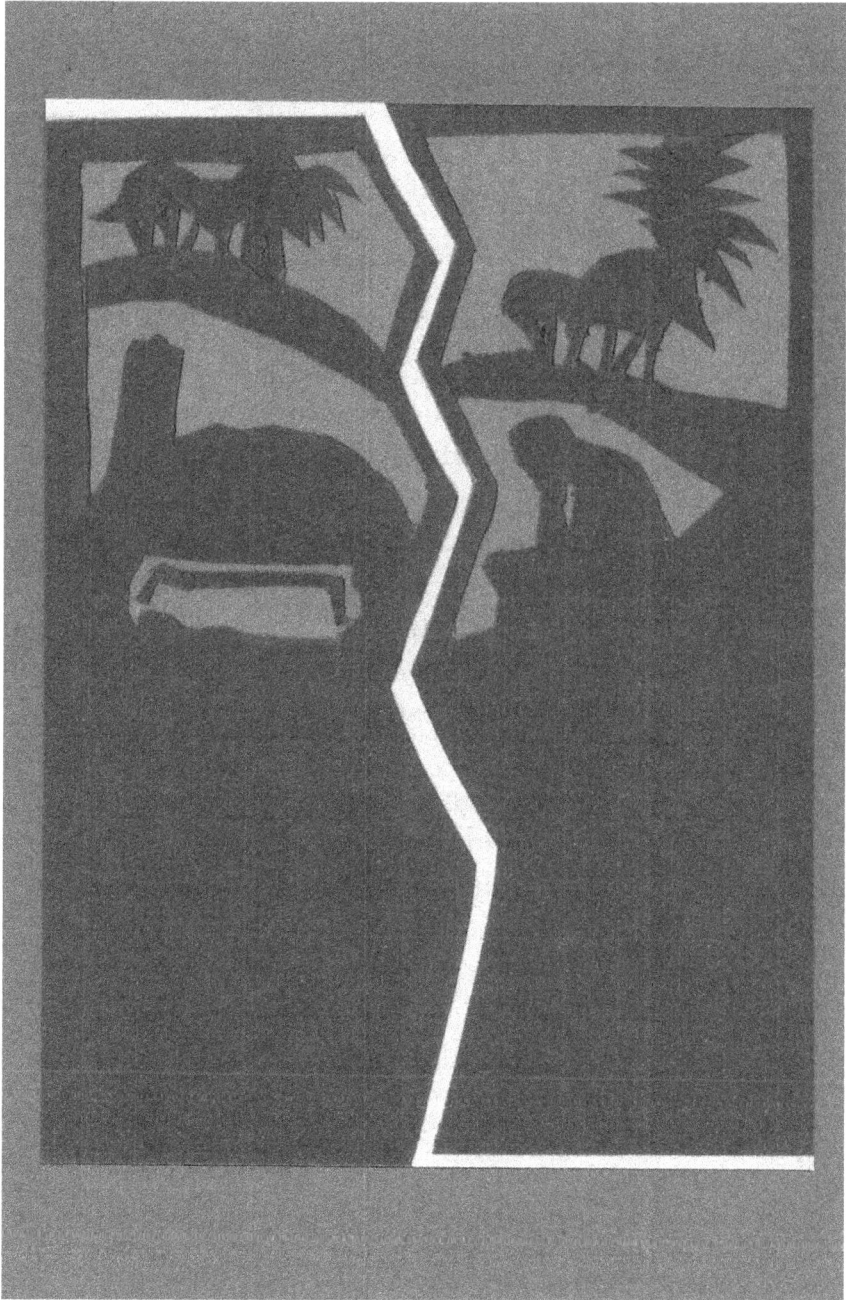

Looking at Your Winter Grave

Are you now a dead thing
      solemn grave?
Once full of flowing light,
      yellow on yellow sun.
Now scrubby bristles hold sway,
      brown and lifeless.
That small fortune that was our lives
      has faded from view,
leaving dried husks, dark thoughts,
      to dim advancing years.
I will have to pull you out, you husks;
      take away your dark presence,
for there are other days other lights
      which will surely renew
the spirit of our lives together, not
      lost but changed now
for the next failing step to eternity:
      Am I so lost, so anxious
that little can fill the space you left?
      Yet I must renew through
Winter's discontent, find light
      in so many lonely hours;
Offer my presence to others' needs
      for renewal is part of life,
if not now the same for me
      but for life's continuity.

Days Without You

In those early days without you
I kept so busy hoping for conversations
to help the understanding of my pain:
       But none came and the pain followed me.

Sometimes I close my eyes and forget
waking with a start to find you nowhere.
Whatever rests outside, darkness stays within
       with no voice to ease your not being.

Expectantly I make my way to others
Hoping conversations might escape convention.
But, alone, realise all our needs are different
       and aloneness is not just for me alone.

Talk of me without you remains untouched
when absence swallows my heart in my mouth;
holding thoughts against the talk of others
       The scale of events unmatched by personal loss

Sometimes the words find a song we can all sing
for humanity, for life, for love for loss as well
reaching across the always space between us:
       Yet loss still haunts me when I am alone.

Now the year has moved its busy days along
and the commonplace of loving dulls your voice;
I feel you all the time somewhere inside me
       Beyond the flatness of the photos that I hold.

Gradually your clothes have been dispersed
through the diaspora of friends and relations:
Withdrawn more the dream once held between us
       to a space of empty shelves and silent drawers.

Mine Is

Mine is no unique condition!
Tell me of other lives taken away
that embroider the hole in the torn
fabric of their lives and now mine:
Children lost to first-time parents;
avalanches of emotion swallowing whole families;
physical disasters and affronts of man to man,
destroying lives and living for some cause:
Lost love, lost lives, needlessly often;
abruptly taken away and lost for ever.

The effects of somewhere, distant leaders
breathing purposes for destruction and mayhem
into ordinary lives across others' homescapes;
Leaving desolation and distress.
So many lost lives seeking their necessary
small survival, rebuilding after and away.

All these recorded happenings,
recurring and far across our world,
shape the perspective in which my
precious loss has to be rated.
We cannot live broken in the debris
of so many lost lives, lost hopes
lost futures, for life endlessly goes on.
Repeating its special atrocities and
reprieves; its destructions and
miraculous resurrections.

Last Fires

Today I burnt some of your old papers:
"Darling auntie, I miss you so much, you
were like a mother to me…" the paper curls
to grey ash but the words hold the air.
"You were always ready to listen…"
and anothr flush and the flames
take you irretrievably away.
"Happy birthday, dear T, hope you…" fades too
as wisps of memory fill the smoking air.
"Dear Mr and Mrs… your esteemed custom"
dates the bill to the time of phones and letters;
There seems little courtesy in today's smoke.
"We really enjoyed seeing you and appreciate
the trouble you…" curls at the corners, fades
and flutters with old photos and cards.

> The conflagration holds its breath
> pages of bank statements resist
> until prodding opens them to the fire
> and lost understanding of your purposes.

"Thank you for all you did for me when…"
The signature crinkles, smokes and is gone.
So many places in this our world, our lives
are reduced by fire and anxious opposites.

I had not thought that some days, friends,
family would end like this, cleaned out, burnt,
lost in the smoke of fading memory: It seems
meaning is too personal, transitory, to suffer
in this way; but, then, the meaning of lives
often does, even when held in photographs
all lost in their last fires.

Who Knows?

Now in my days I might write about you.
Pink petals cover the soil where the rose grows.
The seasons turning will see me through
as the scent of your love lingers. Who knows?

My hand hovers over the empty page, waiting.
Words tumble from the world's woes.
At this time of decisions, futures debating.
My future without you is decided. Who Knows?

Thoughts wander from distraction to distraction.
The air is full of stories; others' highs and lows.
There's a stifling of ideas and loss of action.
Will mindfulness of you revive me? Who knows?

In days, weeks without you, creative thoughts lie;
with quiet moments of reflection my life chose.
Cumulus clouds rise above the blue sky.
Will they cloud my contemplation? Who knows?

I visit the mound regularly that holds you in place.
Tormenting little birds there, magpies and crows.
Reflected in meeting room windows, mine and your
face.
Will this keep me from being submerged? Who knows?

The large birch at the top of the green has died.
Yet the tide of life, like all life, ebbs and flows.
For much of the loss of you, I cried and cried,
for where is the end of each loving thing? Who knows?

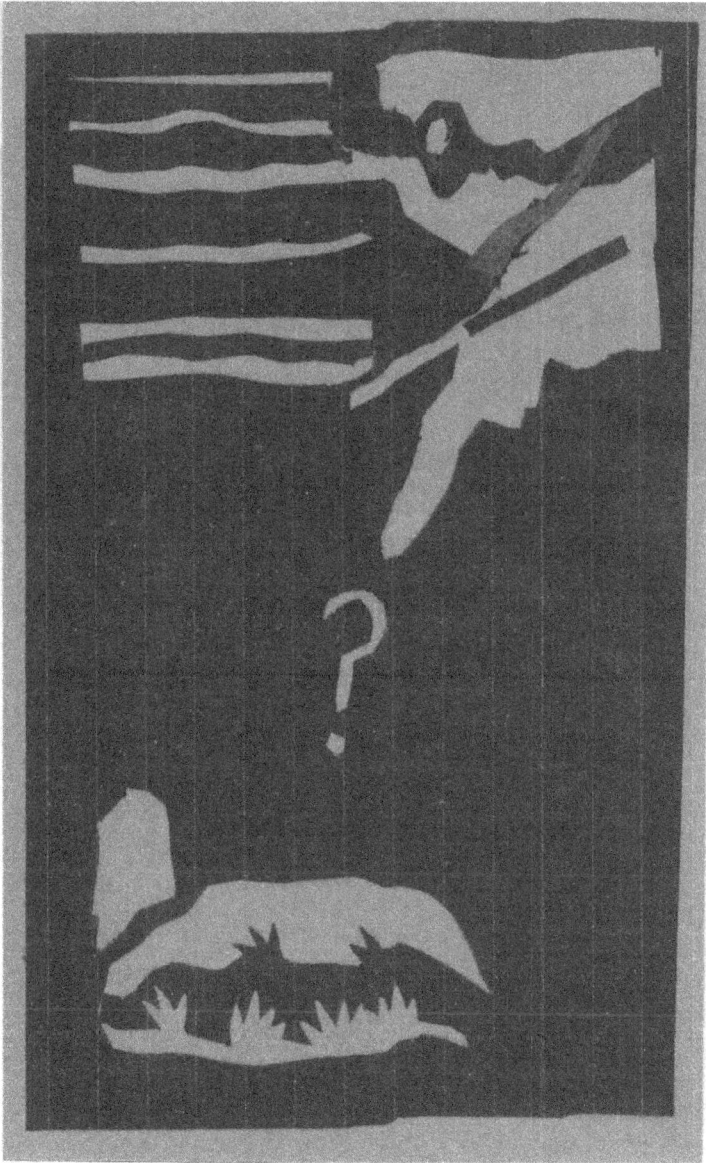

www.ingramcontent.com/pod-product-compliance
Lightning Source LLC
Chambersburg PA
CBHW060602030426
42337CB00019B/3585